Learn to Write Alphabets, Numbers and Shapes

Feera Firza

PARTRIDGE

To order additional copies of this book, contact
Toll Free +65 3165 7531 (Singapore)
Toll Free +60 3 3099 4412 (Malaysia)
orders.singapore@partridgepublishing.com

www.partridgepublishing.com/singapore

This Book belongs to

_____

_____

Let's exercise your fingers.
Trace the dotted lines.

3

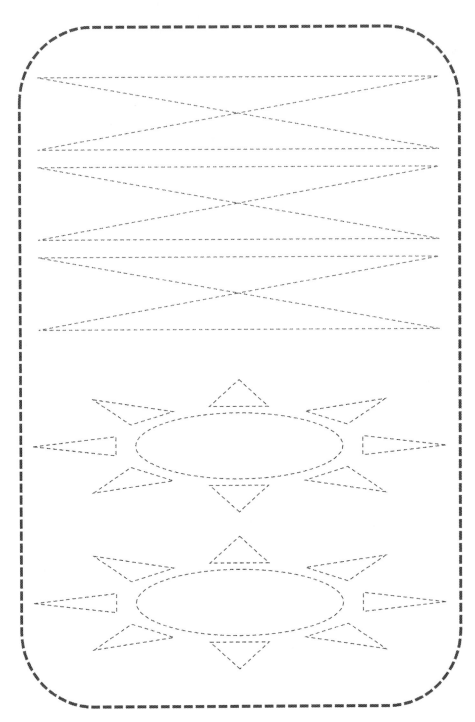

Uppercase And Lowercase Alphabets

Aa Bb Cc Dd

Ee Ff Gg Hh

Ii Jj Kk Ll

Mm Nn Oo Pp

Qq Rr Ss Tt

Uu Vv Ww Xx

Yy Zz

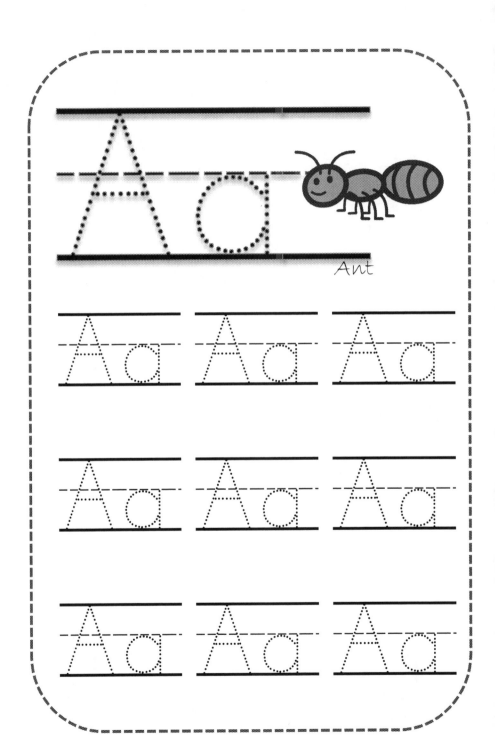

Ant

Aa Aa Aa

Aa Aa Aa

Aa Aa Aa

Aa Aa Aa

Bear

Bb Bb Bb

Bb Bb Bb

Bb Bb Bb

Bb Bb Bb

cat

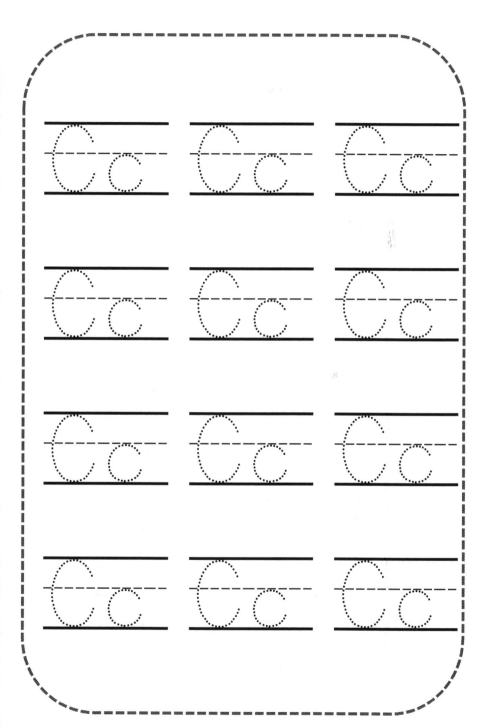

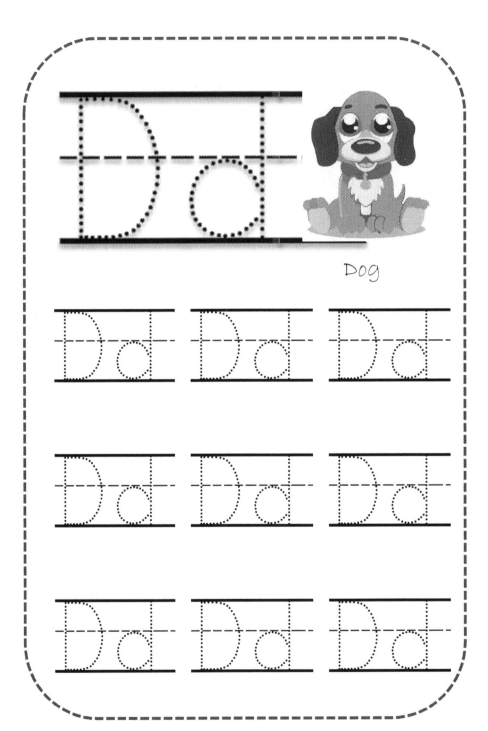

Dog

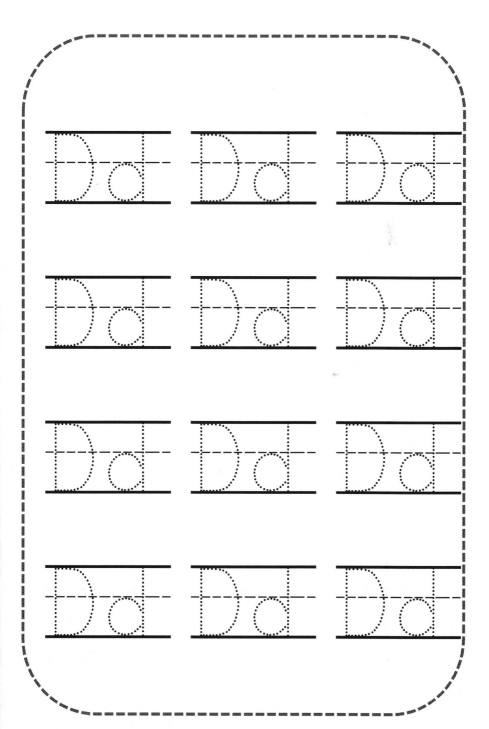

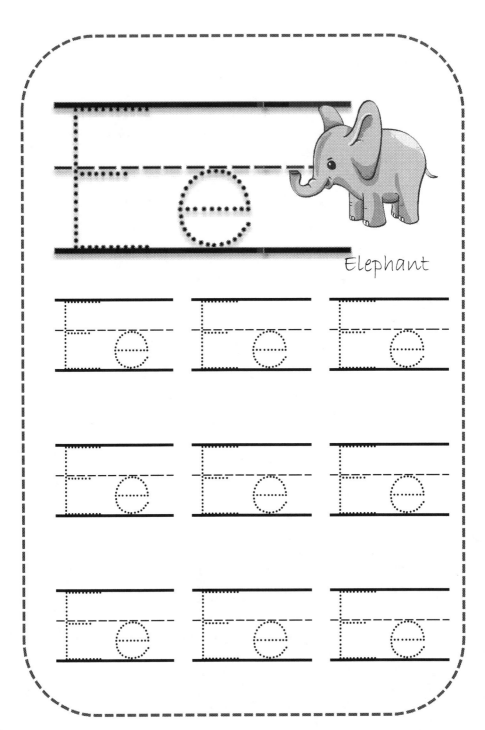

Elephant

14

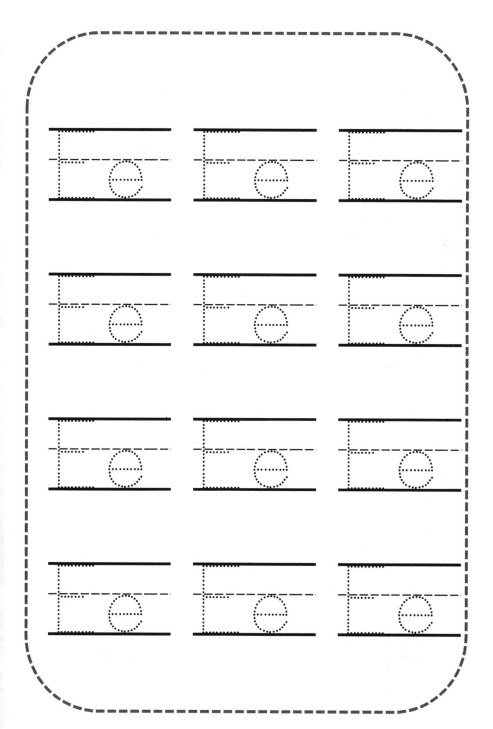

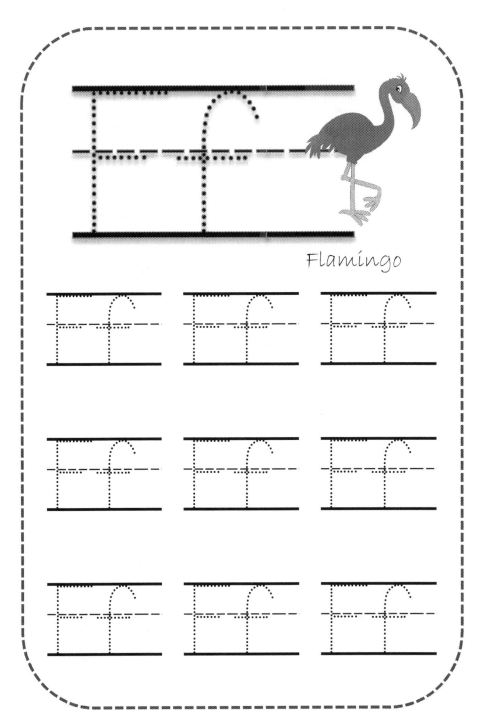

Flamingo

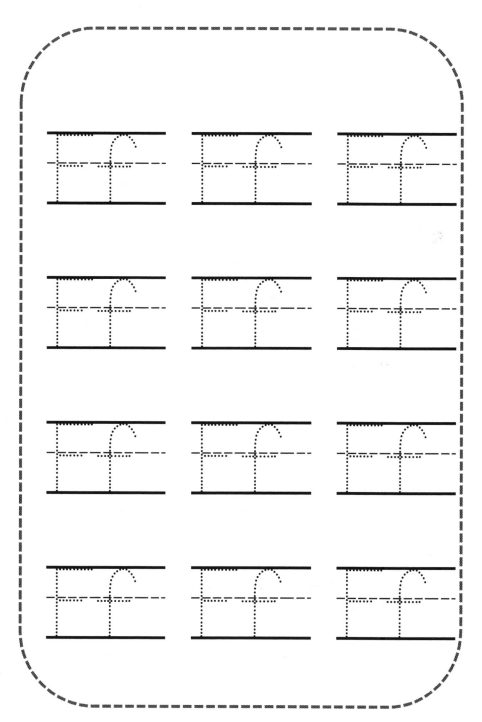

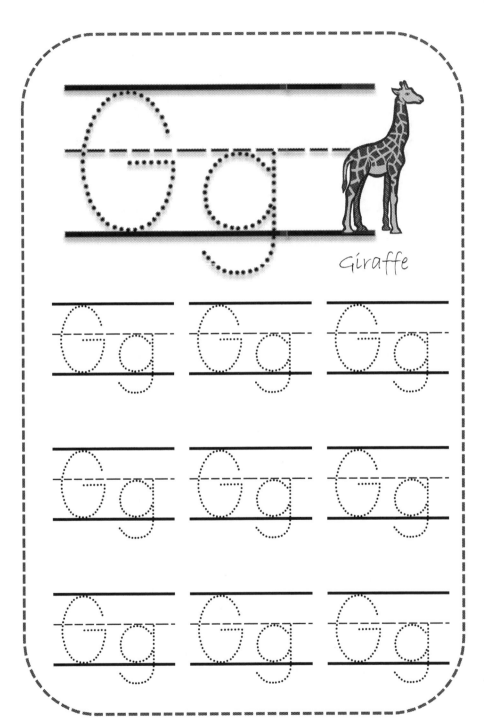

Giraffe

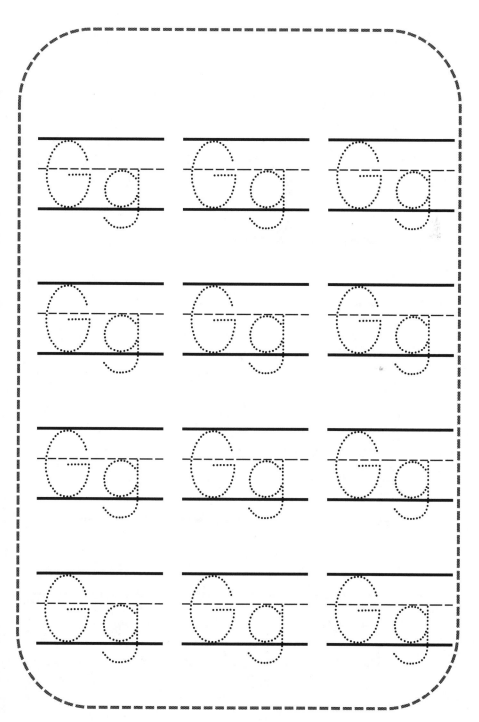

19

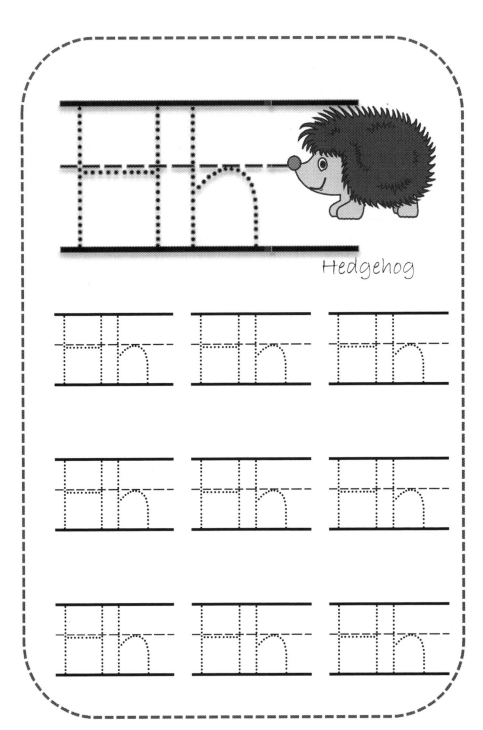

Hedgehog

20

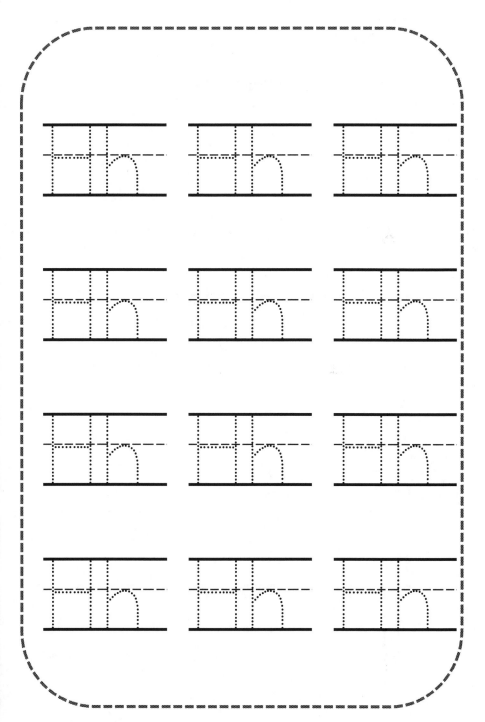

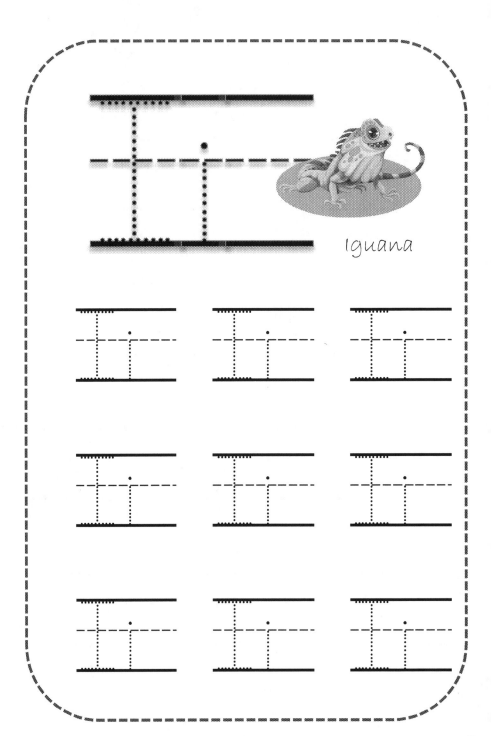

Iguana

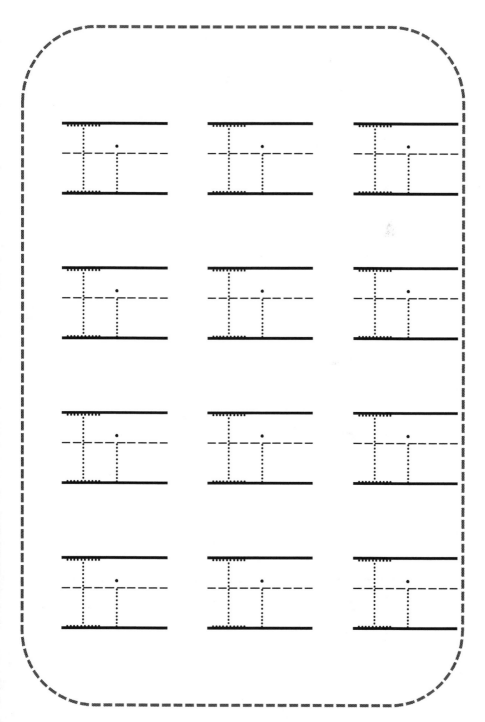

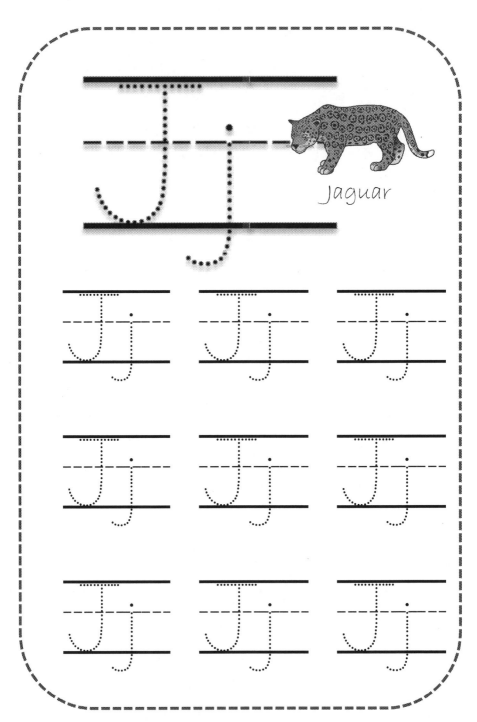

Jaguar

24

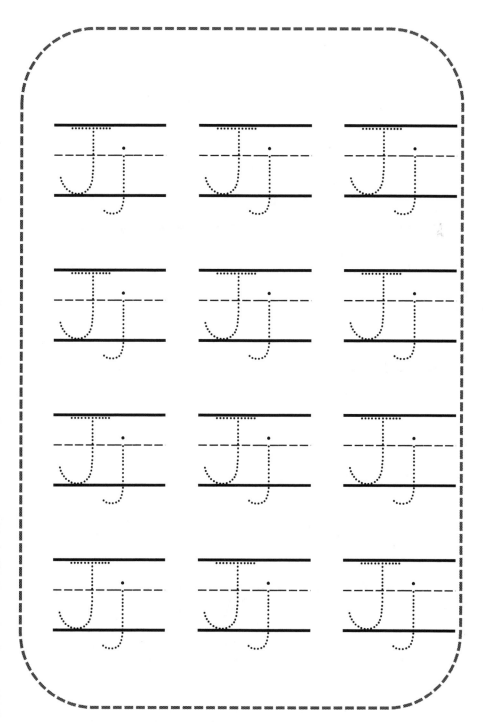

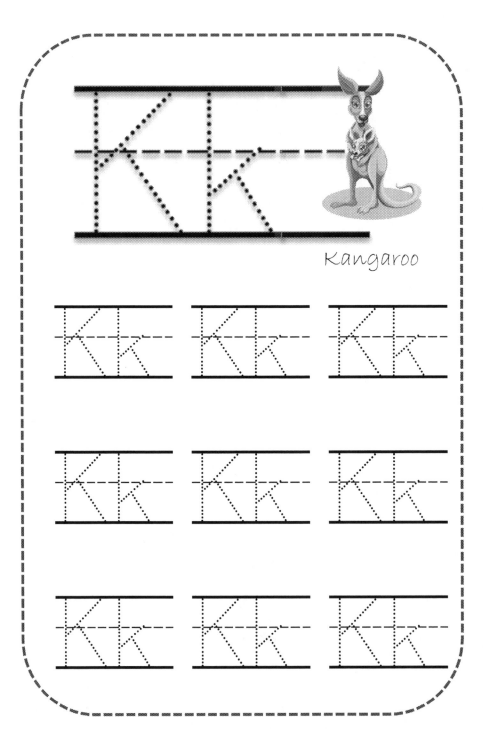

Kangaroo

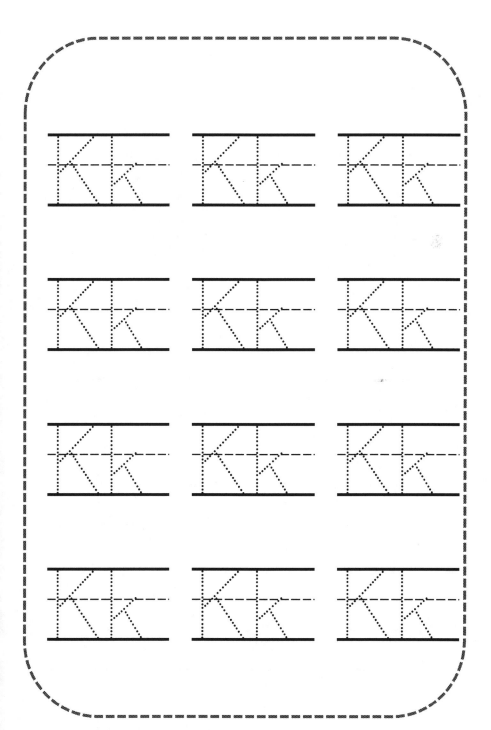

27

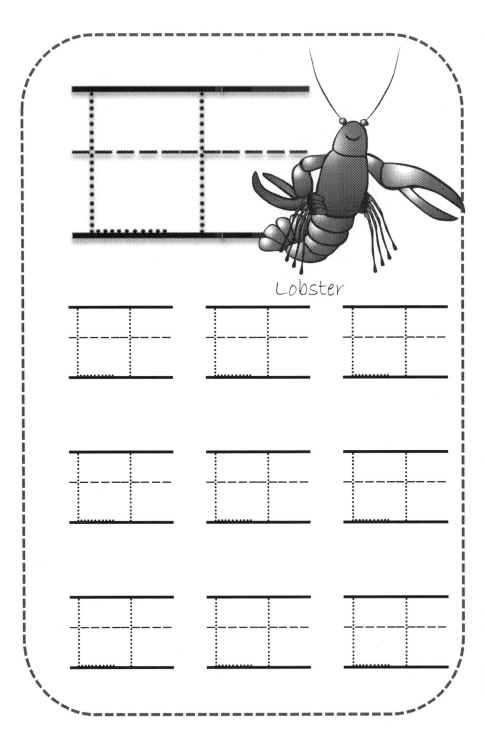

Lobster

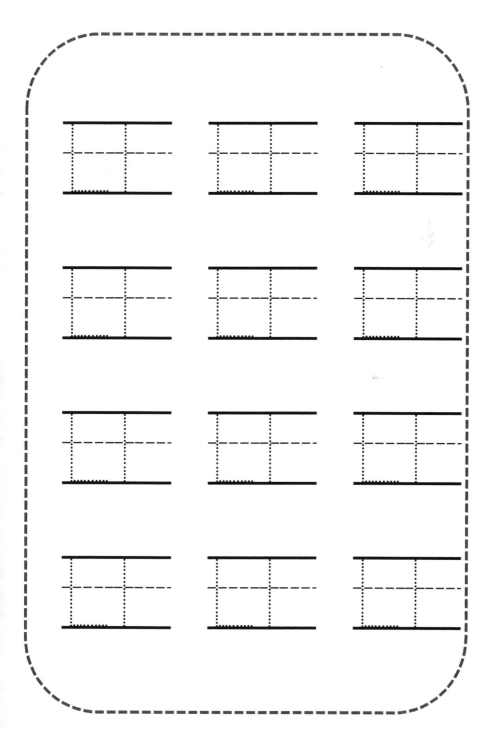

Monkey

30

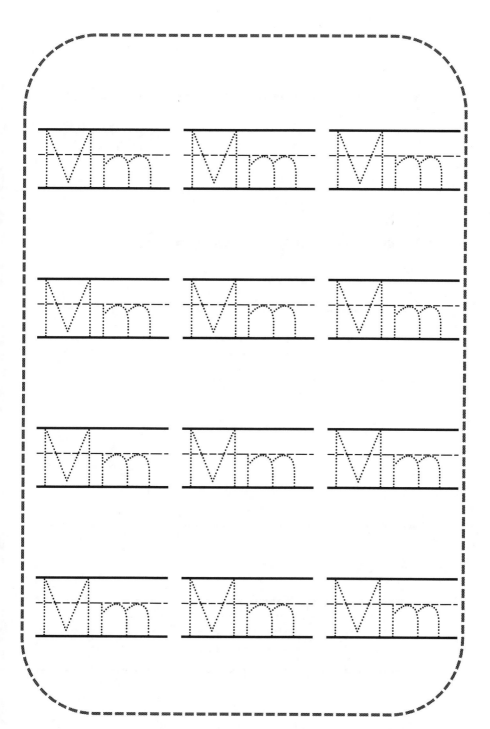

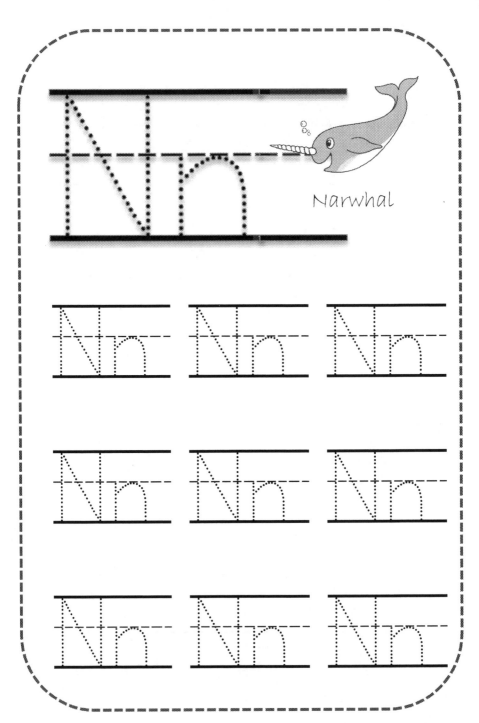

Narwhal

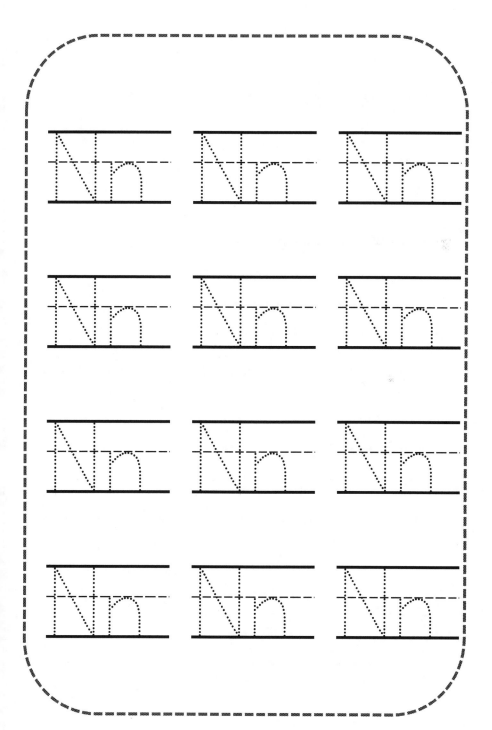

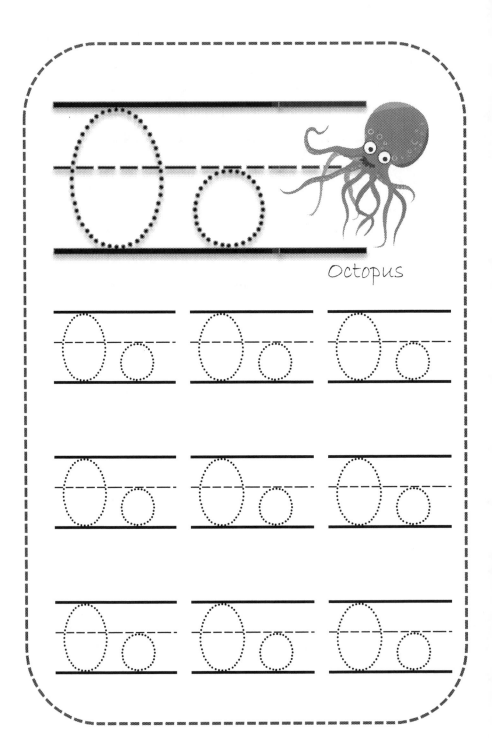

Octopus

34

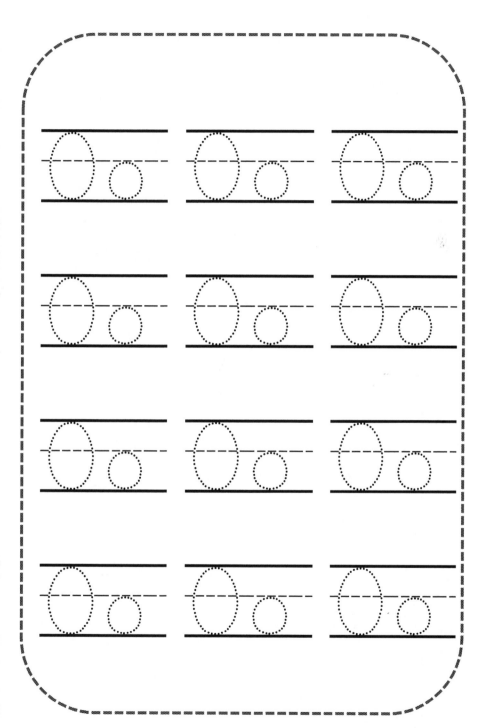

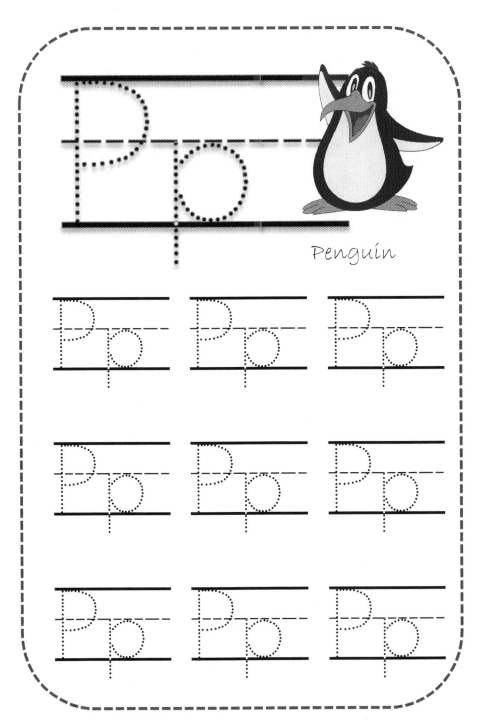

Penguin

36

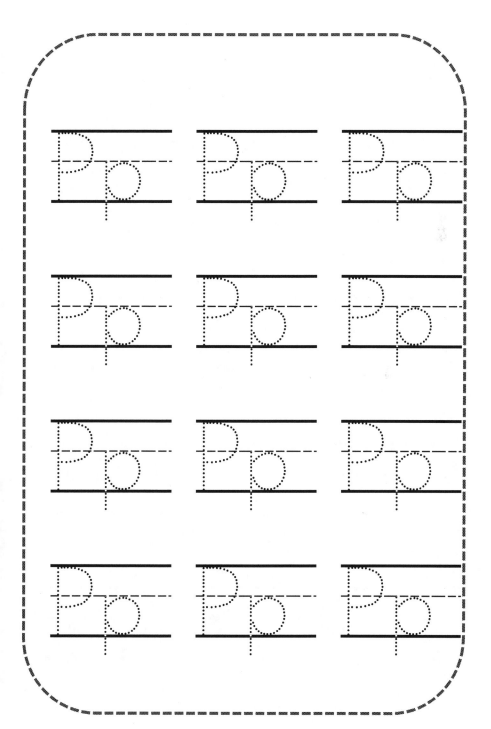

37

Quail

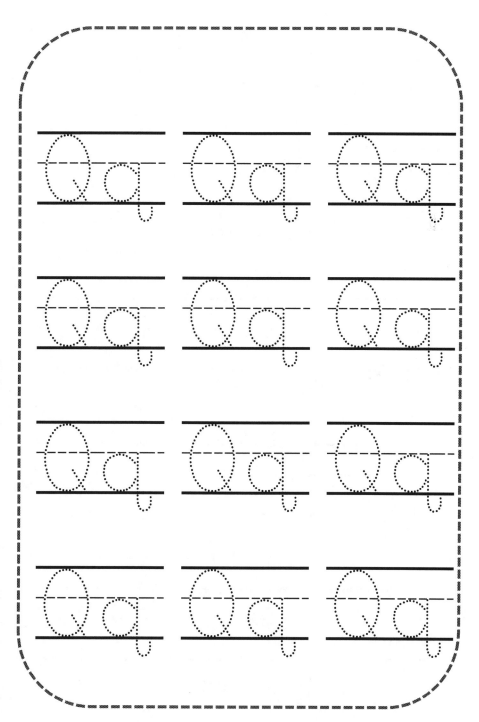

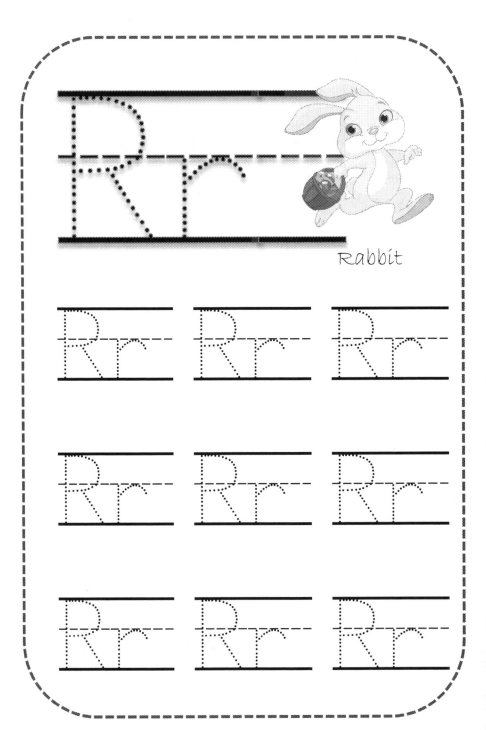

Rabbit

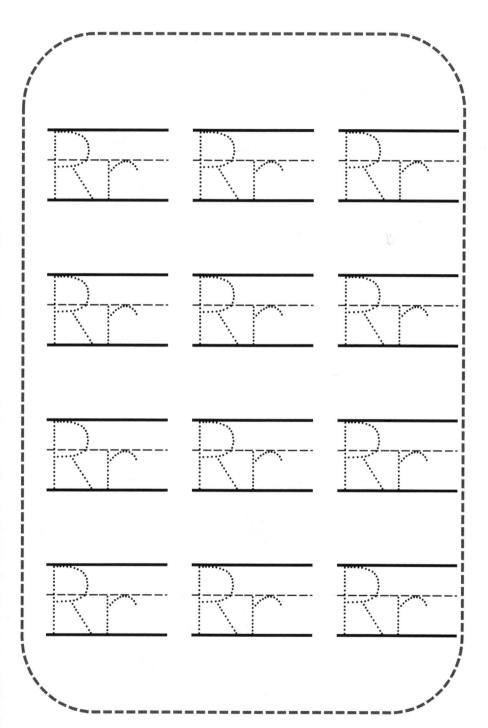

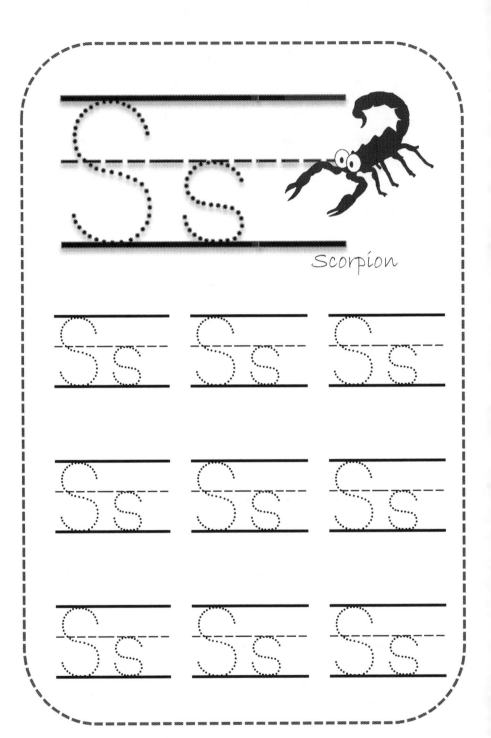

Scorpion

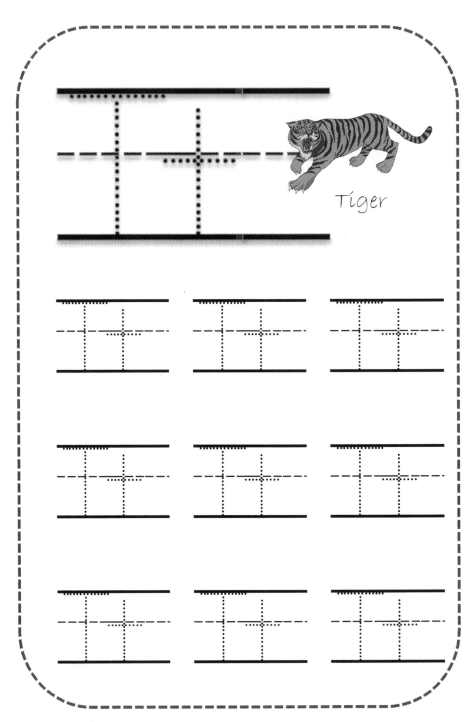

Tiger

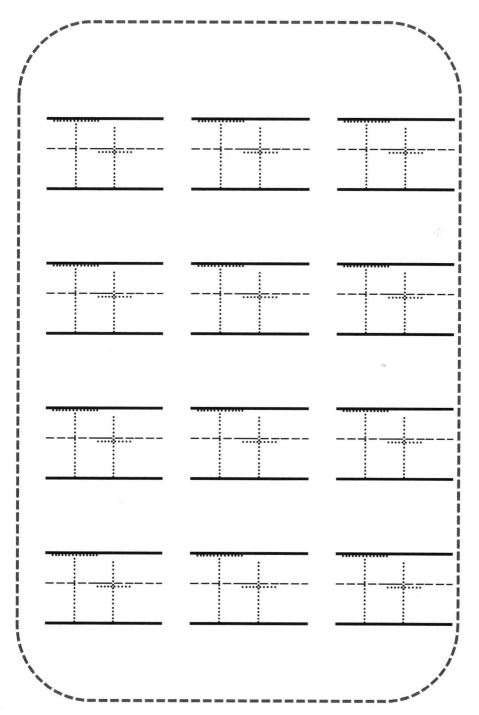

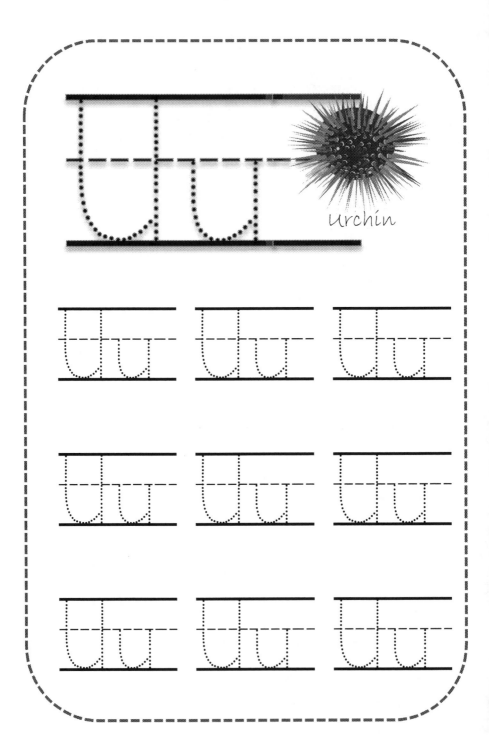

Urchin

46

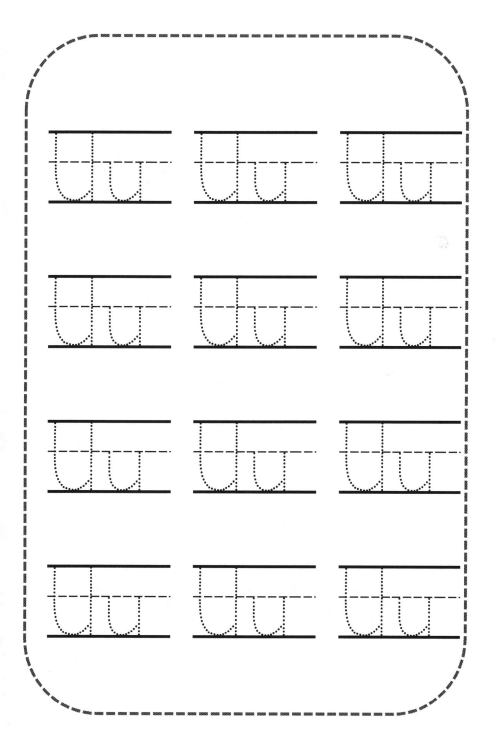

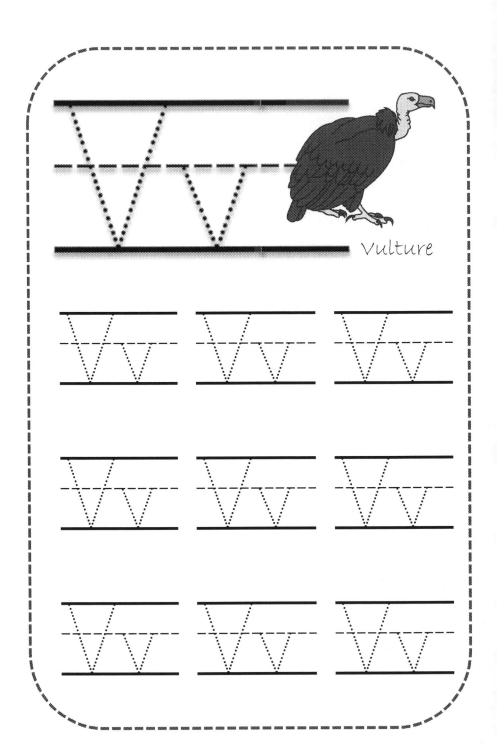

Vulture

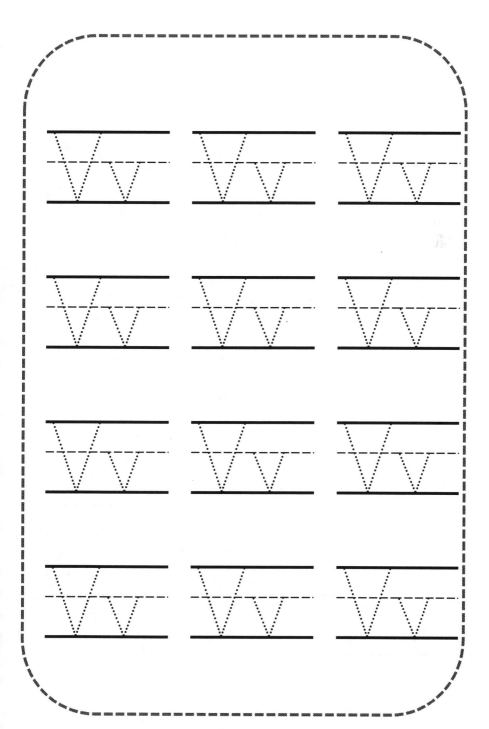

49

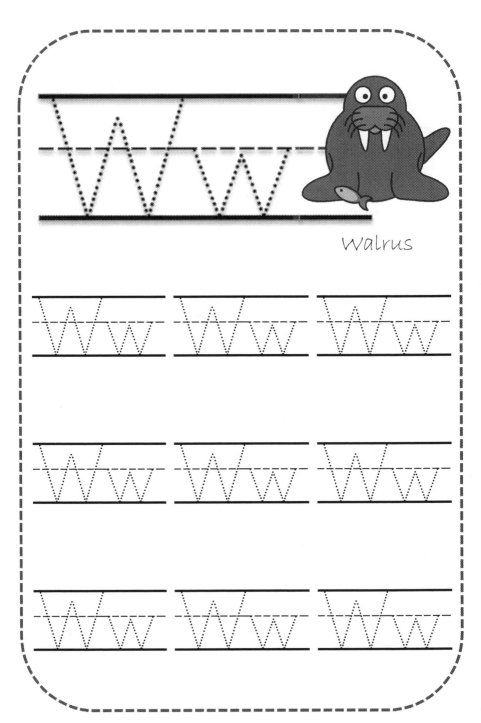

Walrus

50

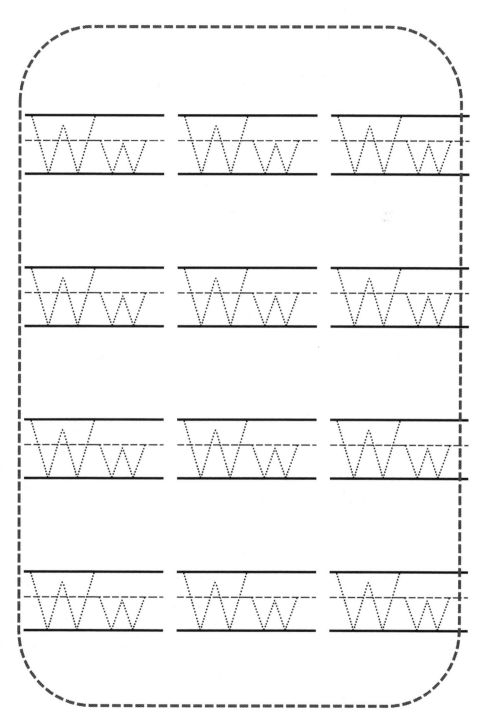

Xantus

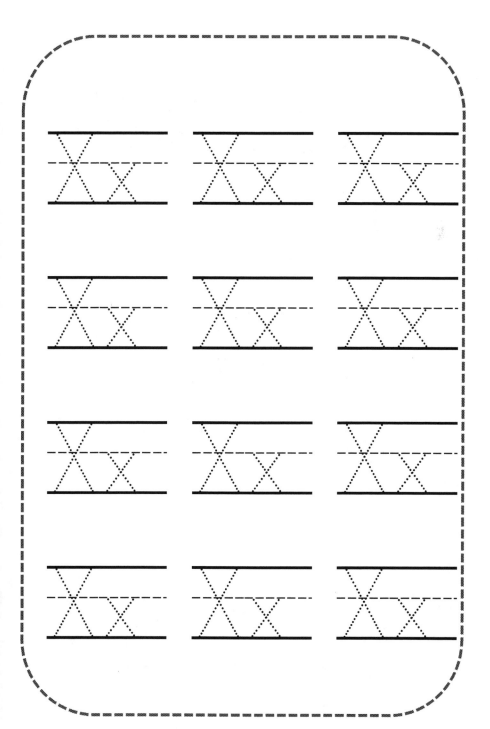

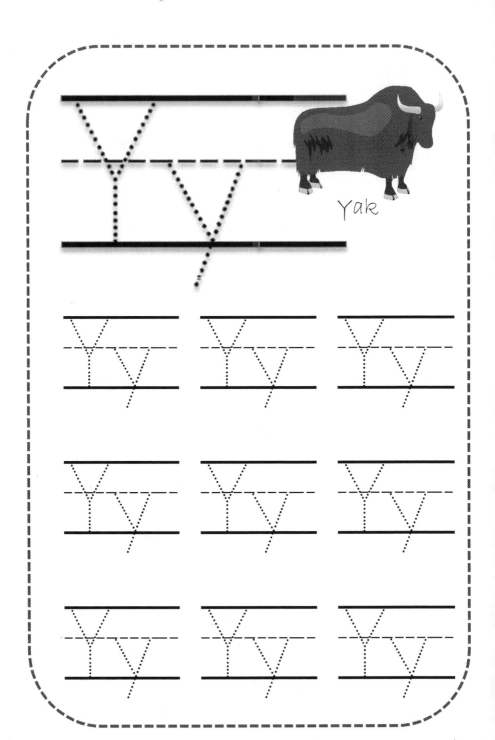

Yak

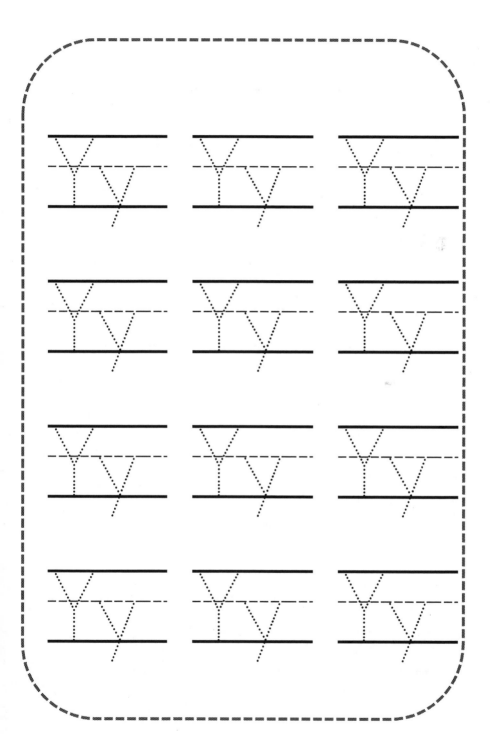

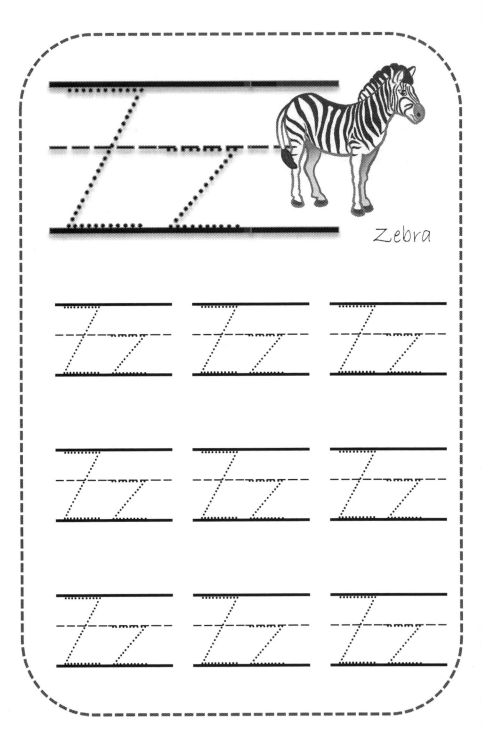

Zebra

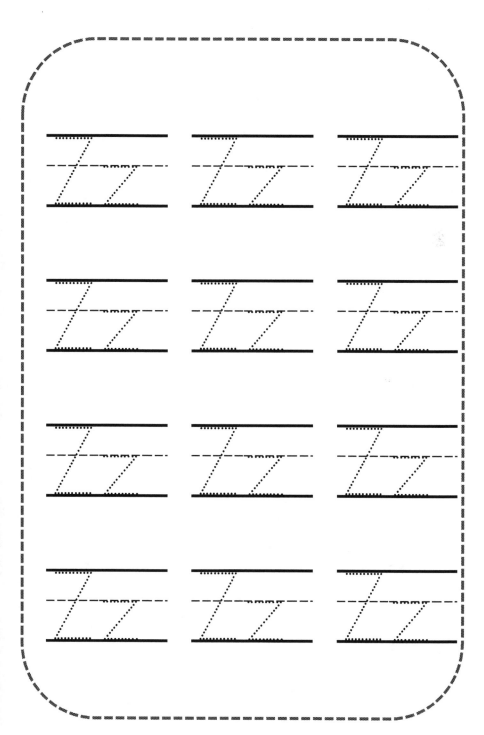

Trace and re-write (uppercase)

FUN   MAN   BAG   MAD

_____   _____   _____   _____

CAT   BAT   FAT   MAT

_____   _____   _____   _____

BAD   RAT   TAB   DAD

_____   _____   _____   _____

Trace and re-write (uppercase)

FAN   YAK   SAD   RED

___   ___   ___   ___

PEN   NET   WET   PET

___   ___   ___   ___

MEN   HOT   TEN   HEN

___   ___   ___   ___

Trace and re-write (uppercase)

LAND   RENT   HAND   LOSS

___   ___   ___   ___

LOST   JAWS   BUS   FIND

___   ___   ___   ___

MESS   BELL   BOLD   MILD

___   ___   ___   ___

Trace and re-write (uppercase)

SUNDAY

_____

MONDAY

_____

TUESDAY

_____

WEDNESDAY

_____

THURSDAY

_____

FRIDAY

_____

SATURDAY

_____

Trace and re-write (uppercase)

JANUARY

_____

MARCH

_____

JUNE

_____

AUGUST

_____

OCTOBER

_____

NOVEMBER

_____

DECEMBER

_____

Choose the correct answer (uppercase) and write it in the box provided. Color the pictures.

| WATERMELON | PEAR | STRAWBERRY |

Choose the correct answer (uppercase) and write it in the box provided. Color the pictures.

APPLE	BANANA	GRAPES

Trace and re-write (lowercase)

hug   yam   bar   hip

tub   zip   cot   dig

dip   bun   had   pop

Trace and re-write (lowercase)

corn   chili   pizza   rice

ruler   book   taxi   lorry

train   juice   pear   vase

Trace and re-write (lowercase)

zebra sheep turtle apple

_____ _____ _____ _____

horse catch pilot lorry

_____ _____ _____ _____

nurse skirt fork ladle

_____ _____ _____ _____

Trace and re-write (lowercase)

winter

summer

elephant

giraffe

bicycle

flower

rabbit

Trace and re-write (lowercase)

pyjamas

_____

pumpkin

_____

eggplant

_____

clock

_____

jacket

_____

watch

_____

glove

_____

Choose the correct answer (lowercase) and write it in the box provided. Color the pictures.

| tree chair kite flower car ship |

Write the alphabets from A to Z in uppercase.

_____   _____   _____   _____   _____

_____   _____   _____   _____   _____

_____   _____   _____   _____   _____

_____   _____   _____   _____   _____

_____   _____   _____   _____   _____

_____

Write the alphabets from a to z in lowercase.

_____   _____   _____   _____   _____

_____   _____   _____   _____   _____

_____   _____   _____   _____   _____

_____   _____   _____   _____   _____

_____   _____   _____   _____   _____

_____

Numbers

1 2 3 4

5 6 7 8

9 10 11 12

13 14 15 16

17 18 19 20

Trace the numbers and words

1   ONE

2   TWO

3   THREE

4   FOUR

5   FIVE

Trace the numbers and words

6   SIX

7   SEVEN

8   EIGHT

9   NINE

10   TEN

Trace the numbers and words

11   ELEVEN

12   TWELVE

13   THIRTEEN

14   FOURTEEN

15   FIFTEEN

Trace the numbers and words

16 SIXTEEN

17 SEVENTEEN

18 EIGHTEEN

19 NINETEEN

20 TWENTY

Trace the dotted lines

1 2 3 4 5

1 2 3 4 5

1 2 3 4 5

1 2 3 4 5

1 2 3 4 5

Trace the dotted lines

6 7 8 9 10

6 7 8 9 10

6 7 8 9 10

6 7 8 9 10

6 7 8 9 10

Trace the dotted lines

11   12   13   14   15

11   12   13   14   15

11   12   13   14   15

11   12   13   14   15

11   12   13   14   15

Trace the dotted lines

16 17 18 19 20

16 17 18 19 20

16 17 18 19 20

16 17 18 19 20

16 17 18 19 20

Count the shapes and write the
correct answer in the box provided.

Count the animals and write the correct answer in the box provided.

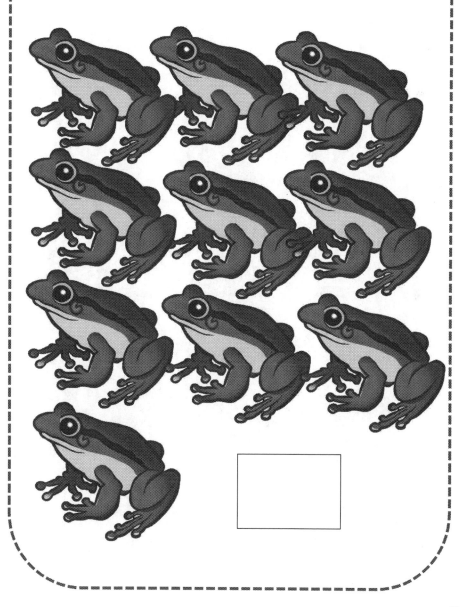

Count the animals and write the correct answer in the box provided.

Count the animals and write the
correct answer in the box provided.

Count the dots and write the correct answer in the box provided.

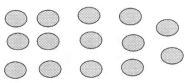

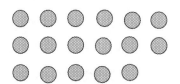

Fill in boxes with the numbers that come before and after the middle number.

	5				11	
	8				10	
	4				14	
	2				18	
	6				16	
	9				13	
	7				15	
	3				17	

Fill in the missing numbers accordingly.

| 1 | | | 4 | |

| 6 | | | | 10 |

| 11 | | 13 | | 15 |

| 16 | | | | 20 |

Write the numbers 1 to 20

_____   _____   _____   _____   _____

_____   _____   _____   _____   _____

_____   _____   _____   _____   _____

_____   _____   _____   _____   _____

Shapes

CIRCLE

SQUARE

DIAMOND

PENTAGON

TRIANGLE

OVAL

HEART

HEXAGON

RECTANGLE

Trace the dotted lines and color the shapes.

Trace the dotted lines and color the shapes.

Trace the dotted lines and color the shapes.

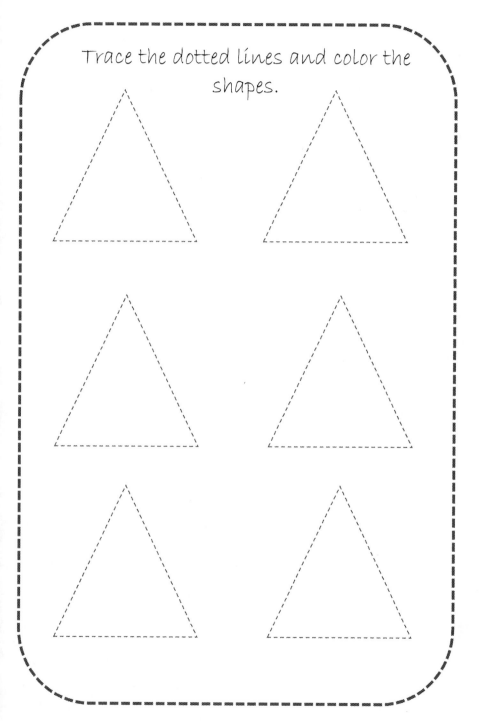

Trace the dotted lines and color the shapes.

Trace the dotted lines and color the shapes.

Trace the dotted lines and color the shapes.

Trace the dotted lines and color the shapes.

Trace the dotted lines and color the shapes.

Trace the dotted lines and color the shapes.

Let's draw using the shapes.
Trace the dotted lines and color it.

Draw a flower using your favorite shapes.

Let's draw using the shapes.
Trace the dotted lines and color it.

Draw a house using your favorite shapes.

Let's draw using the shapes.
Trace the dotted lines and color it.

Draw a train or a car using your favorite shapes.

Let's draw using the shapes.
Trace the dotted lines and color it.

Draw a rocket using your favorite shapes.

Printed in the United States
by Baker & Taylor Publisher Services

~